For Molly, Rainer and Rohan.
Thank you my darlings.

Spiral Orchard Publications

First published in Great Britain 2024
This paperback edition was first published 2024
Copyright 2024 text and illustration by Sophie Pryce-Baxter

The right of Sophie Pryce-Baxter to be identified as the author and illustrator of this work has been asserted by her in accordance with The Copyright, Designs and Patents Act 1988

No part of this publication may be reproduced, stored in a retrieval system or transmitted in any form or by any means without prior written permission of the publisher Spiral Orchard Publications.

This is a work of fiction All characters, organisations and events portrayed in this picture book are either products of the author's imagination or are usedfictitiously. No resemblance is intended to living or dead persons.

The CIP catalogue record for this book is available from the British Library.

ISBN: 978-1-0685435-1-7 (hardcover)
ISBN: 978-1-0685435-0-0 (paperback)

The Adventures of Gertie Gillytwig

Tricks 'n' Treats

Written and illustrated by

Sophie Pryce-Baxter

In a little cottage at the end of a twisty, bumpy old lane, there lives a witch called Gertie Gillytwig.

Gertie is a real witch. Her nose isn't warty, and her hair isn't green. However, she does love her pointy hats. And even though she flies on her broomstick, she prefers to ride on her bicycle. Besides, Rhubarb hates flying.

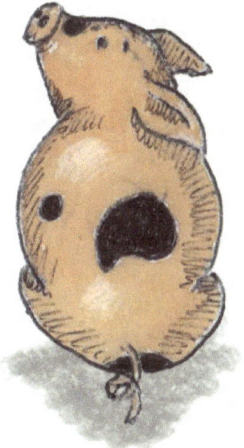

Instead of a black cat,
a bat, or even a toad,
as other witches prefer,
Gertie has a pot-bellied pig.

Now and then, a pixie or a fairy, or sometimes even goblins, come to her for help.

Even though Gertie is very good at magic, she only uses it when she has to. You see, spells can go wrong, as she found out once with a goblin! But I won't go into that now!

So, most of her time is spent growing herbs in her garden and boiling potions. And she bakes an apple pie every Wednesday with a crusty pastry top.

But sometimes, just sometimes, she has adventures.

I'll tell you about one right now.

It was the last day of October, and Gertie was getting ready for the Halloween party.

The toffee apples were cooling, and Gertie had put on her best dress and had even brushed her hair. She was about to slide her feet into her yellow welly boots when she heard a tiny tap at the door.

Rhubarb excitedly ran over, but when Gertie opened it, she was surprised to see a puffed-out fairy instead of the children trick-or-treating.

Glittering specks of fairy dust were scattering everywhere as she flittered around.

Her cheeks were bright purple, the same colour as her dress, and she was round like a plum.

"How can I help you?" Gertie said in her best witchy cackle.

The little fairy took a few gulps of air. "My name is Plum," she panted between sobs. "It's my turn to make sure all the sweets don't run out on Samhain." she cried. (That's what fairies call Halloween). "It's the most important job of all."

She searched through her pockets, pulled out a tiny handkerchief, and blew her nose loudly.

"Come in and sit by the fire and tell me everything." (Gertie decided it was best to use her normal voice now; otherwise, she'd get a sore throat).

The sugar plum fairy slowly floated down and sat on the edge of the chair.

"Well, I put the Never-ending Sweets bag in a safe place, but when I went to check on it, it was gone." she sobbed again. "Now all the sweets will run out. OH!" Plum wept into her already soggy handkerchief.

Rhubarb had come to see what was going on but kept wondering if the fairy tasted of sugar.

"But I did find this." The fairy held up a tiny green slipper with a small apple perched on its tip. "I think it belongs to the Crab Apple Fairy."

Gertie took the tiny shoe. "I have an idea," she said as she walked over to a tall cupboard and pulled out a large book. She placed it on the table and started to flick through the pages.

"Here it is," she said.

Plum flew over and saw the heading:

'Missing: Never-ending Sweet Bag Spell.'

"Now, let's see... We need some fairy dust."

Plum pulled out a small bag from one of her tiny pockets. "Will this do?"

Gertie nodded. "Now, all we need is a twig—hazel would be the best," she said. "Follow me."

Picking up the spell book, Gertie led Plum into a room full of dusty, cobweb-covered shelves. Plum flew up and looked at all the different coloured bottles. One bright green bottle was labelled: **'Explosive!'**

Then she saw a shiny globe that seemed to sparkle. Unable to stop herself, Plum flew to the top shelf and glared at the round object.

The colours swirled before her eyes,

but before she could make out the image coming to life, she turned as Gertie called out.

"Found it!" said Gertie, jumping up with a forked twig.

Gertie took the hazel twig, the tiny green slipper, and the pinch of fairy dust over to the large bubbling pot and plopped everything into the brew.

Rhubarb had decided to join them; she thought something interesting might happen.

Standing over the cauldron, Gertie read from the book.

"Hocus pocus, tiddly tum,
help us find what belongs to the fairy Plum."

The gloop in the cauldron changed colour, and the flames turned bright pink. Suddenly, a puff of glittery green smoke exploded out of the pot, making everyone cough and splutter as it filled the room.

Next, a humming noise came from the black bowl; it grew louder as the pot began to shake. Gertie, Plum, and Rhubarb all stood back.

Now hovering above the cauldron, the hazel twig twitched and jerked as small green leaves grew like feathers.

Then it shot out of the fireplace and whizzed around, crashing into the bottles that exploded in puffs of coloured smoke.

Rhubarb scurried out of the room (as much as a pot-bellied pig could scurry) and hid under her blanket.

Gertie ducked as the twig shot out of the door. "We have to follow that twig!" Gertie grabbed her purple hat and stripy scarf as she rushed to the garden.

Reaching the little shed, Gertie tugged at the creaky door, pulled out her trusty yellow bicycle, and plopped Rhubarb into the front basket.

Plum flew up beside them. "You'll never keep up in that," the fairy said. "This will help."

Before Gertie could stop her, Plum sprinkled a handful of fairy dust over the yellow bike.

"Oh, dear!" Gertie didn't mind flying, but Rhubarb wasn't fond of heights. Hence, the saying, 'pigs might fly', means they never do, for precisely that reason.

As the bicycle started to rise, Rhubarb squealed. Gertie quickly found a little apple in her coat pocket and stuffed it into the quivering pig's mouth.

"Which way did it go?" Gertie asked.

"There!" shouted Plum. "Follow me." She flew off as Gertie peddled frantically to keep up.

As the night started to creep in, they flew over Peasham (pronounced Peas-ham, but you must say it quietly, or Rhurbarb will get upset).

They were excited to see the lit lanterns at every door.

As the moon rose behind her, Gertie could make out the woodland in the distance and watched as the twig drifted to the ground.

She pushed on the handlebars, the wheels touched down, and Gertie slammed on the brakes before skidding to a stop; Rhubarb's apple flew out of her mouth.

"The spell's run out," said Gertie, picking up the twig. "But I think it was going in there."

"We can't go in there!" said Plum in a quiet, shaky voice.

"Why are you whispering?" whispered Gertie.

"This is Dodge Wood," Plum explained.

The trees creaked and cracked as they walked through the dark woods.

Then, a light flickered from the shadows. Rhubarb's snout sniffed the air, and she followed the pretty, shimmering glow.

"Was that a will-o-wisp?" Gertie asked worriedly. "Which way did it go?" Gertie searched through the gloomy forest to find her.

Before she could light the candle Gertie found in her pocket, she went hurtling to the ground. Plum screamed and landed with a thump beside her. Gertie spat out the soggy leaves.

"Who did that?" she asked crossly.

Someone snickered.

Gertie held up the candle. She quickly muttered,

"Light my way as if it were day."

And the candle burst into a blue flame.

"Did you just push us over?" Gertie asked. "That wasn't very nice!" She held the candle higher, which had changed to a green glow.

The tree stopped laughing. It hung its head low, as best a tree could, and said, "Sorry."

"Maybe you can help us?" Gertie asked. "We're looking for the Crab Apple fairy."

The tree looked thoughtful, "There is the fairy lair." He whispered as if he was scared. A heavy branch slowly lifted and cracked as it pointed. "It's that way."

With the candle floating before them, now with a pink flame, Plum flew closely behind. Soon, they heard a tinkling sound from ahead.

"That must be it," said Plum as she shot off.

"Wait for me!" Just as Gertie was about to go after Plum, she noticed the will-o-wisp; Rhurbarb was in hot pursuit; the will-o-wisp looked nervous. Gertie picked up her pig quickly and ran after the fairy.

Gertie stopped at the edge of the most beautiful place she'd ever seen and lowered the wriggling pig to the ground.

Flowers bloomed as sunlight beamed down on a circle of fairies playing music.

But as Gertie blinked and looked again, one fairy banged on a stone. Other fairies tried to sing along, which Gertie imagined would sound twinkly and magical, but it was more like someone had a very bad throat.

This must be the fairy lair.

Gertie blew out the now purple flame.

As she did, the music suddenly stopped, and the fairies started to scream and fly away. Rhubarb ran into the clearing and began to lick them.

Gertie noticed a fairy who had hidden under a large red toadstool.

In the chaos, Gertie hadn't noticed the two fairies at first, playing tug of war with the sweets pouring from the bag. One fairy was green from head to toe, and Gertie noticed the fairy was missing a shoe.

"Give it back!" Plum shouted.

"No, I want to do it." The other screamed.

The bag was pulled this way and that until the string snapped. The Crab Apple fairy flew through the air and landed in the mound of sweets. Rhubarb moved in.

Gertie and Plum gasped.

"YUCH! That was DISGUSTING!"

screamed the Crab Apple Fairy after Rhubarb spat her out.

Gertie laughed as Plum started to giggle.

"That serves you right," said Plum, who suddenly looked upset as she looked up at the night sky through the trees. "There won't be time to give out all the sweets now. Halloween's ruined!"

Gertie looked at the two miserable fairies. "I have an idea." She said. "If you are willing to share, you'll get the job done in double the time. What do you say?" Gertie waited for an answer.

"All right, I'm willing to, but only if the Crab Apple fairy behaves herself."

"I will," she answered quietly. I've always wanted to give out the sweets; I wasn't going to keep them, honestly!"

As the two fairies flew off with the bag, Gertie smiled. All the children would get their sweets, and the fairies could share the job of handing them out.

And if Gertie hurried, she'd even have time to go to her party, though Rhubarb may not want any more sweets for a while or fly again in her magical bicycle.

The End.

www.ingramcontent.com/pod-product-compliance
Lightning Source LLC
Chambersburg PA
CBHW041536040426
42446CB00002B/115